SO YOU WANNA BE

An Artist

HILARIE STATON

Rourke Educational Media
rourkeeducationalmedia.com

Before & After Reading Activities

Before Reading:

Building Academic Vocabulary and Background Knowledge

Before reading a book, it is important to tap into what your child or students already know about the topic. This will help them develop their vocabulary, increase their reading comprehension, and make connections across the curriculum.

1. *Look at the cover of the book. What will this book be about?*
2. *What do you already know about the topic?*
3. *Let's study the Table of Contents. What will you learn about in the book's chapters?*
4. *What would you like to learn about this topic? Do you think you might learn about it from this book? Why or why not?*
5. *Use a reading journal to write about your knowledge of this topic. Record what you already know about the topic and what you hope to learn about the topic.*
6. *Read the book.*
7. *In your reading journal, record what you learned about the topic and your response to the book.*
8. *After reading the book complete the activities below.*

Content Area Vocabulary

Read the list. What do these words mean?

certificate
conventions
deadline
freelancers
galleries
network
publisher
sequential
specialized
technical
techniques

After Reading:

Comprehension and Extension Activity

After reading the book, work on the following questions with your child or students in order to check their level of reading comprehension and content mastery.

1. *What does an animator do? (Summarize)*
2. *What are some ways networking can help people find jobs? (Infer)*
3. *What is a freelancer? (Asking Questions)*
4. *What types of art do you enjoy creating? (Text to Self Connection)*
5. *How can a college degree help someone become a professional artist? (Asking Questions)*

Extension Activity

If you are interested in a career as a professional artist, it's never too soon to start creating a portfolio. Organize the best work you have made so far. Then make a point to add a new piece to it regularly. You can organize it by month or year as you create more and more. This will also help you see the progress you make as an artist!

Table of Contents

An Artist's Life

Hobby and career artists have two things in common. They are passionate about what they do and they are creative. They love to create art.

Successful artists must depend on themselves to grow, to search out what they like and don't like, to learn the basics, and to find jobs. Being an artist isn't easy.

Some earn their pay outside of art and do art as a hobby. Others are employees of a company and do a specific type of art. Some become **freelancers**. Freelancers are usually hired to do one job at a time and must continually search for the next job. They often work for several companies.

PRO ADVICE

"I'M STILL PRACTICING AND GETTING BETTER. I ALSO LOOK AT A LOT OF VIDEOS ON YOUTUBE .... AND WHEN I MEET WITH OTHER ARTISTS, I'M NOT AFRAID TO ASK QUESTIONS. IF YOU THINK YOU KNOW EVERYTHING, YOU'LL NEVER LEARN ANYTHING." JERRY CRAFT, COMIC BOOK AND GRAPHIC NOVEL ARTIST

Most professional artists have a studio where they work, but they probably started drawing someplace like the kitchen table. At first, their tools were probably paper and pencil. Depending on their interests, they might have moved into using paints, a drawing board, or a computer tablet with **specialized** programs.

Artists continually practice their skills to improve. Although some careers depend on drawing skills more than others, all artists need the basics.

FAST FACT

A student who participates in the arts is four times more likely to be recognized for academic achievement, according to americansforthearts.org.

PRO ADVICE

"DRAW, DRAW, DRAW, THEN DRAW SOME MORE. BUT DON'T JUST DRAW CHARACTERS THAT YOU'VE MADE UP. TRY TO DRAW FROM LIFE. DRAW REAL PEOPLE AND PLACES. HAVE FUN DRAWING THINGS THAT ARE EASY, BUT PRACTICE DRAWING THINGS THAT ARE HARD, LIKE HANDS OR HORSES. AND STUDY ARTISTS THAT YOU LIKE, PROFESSIONAL ARTISTS WHO ARE WELL PAID FOR THEIR WORK." JUNE BRIGMAN, COMIC BOOK AND COMIC STRIP ARTIST

Most artists also need to get along with a team of people who help create the art. This might be the director of a movie or the person who letters their comic book.

Many artists **network** to get new jobs or to sell their artwork. Some attend art fairs or comic **conventions,** while others post their work on the Internet.

The director is the leader of the team that decides how a movie will look.

PRO ADVICE

"Connect with people in your community who are interested in the arts. Join local art organizations, and have goals for yourself. Make time to paint every day, even when you have a job which pays the bills. It's critical to have self-discipline as a painter, because the more you work, the faster you develop your own personal style or voice. And finally, follow your instinct, and believe in yourself." Karen O'Neil, fine artist and art teacher

BREAKING IN

The most important thing for artists wanting to work in a particular field is to get their work in front of those doing the hiring. Although you can post your work on the Internet, the main way to get hired is by networking. Some artists join organizations, such as the Graphic Artists Guild or the National Cartoonists Society, to develop contacts. Other artists might work with an agent to help them find freelance assignments. At conventions, new artists attend workshops and meet with editors and established artists.

Fine Artists

Fine artists draw, paint, or create sculptures to communicate an idea, to show beauty, or even sadness.

Fine artists must be creative. They must search for what inspires them and for the best way to express what they hope to communicate.

They must be self-motivated to set their own goals and to decide how to reach them. They don't usually try to meet expectations set by other people. If they want to sell their art, they must get it in front of buyers at art shows, **galleries**, or on the Internet.

PRO ADVICE

"I have worked at museums and for painting and frame conservators and later taught art from middle school to college levels. All the while, I kept developing my painting skills by making art and showing locally." Cindy Dill, a fine artist

An illustrator is an artist whose art is created for someplace specific, such as a magazine, book, advertisement, or greeting card.

Award-winning Sam Lloyd both writes and illustrates her children's books. She has a university degree in illustration.

POLICE SKETCH ARTISTS

These illustrators must listen carefully to a person describing someone. The artist draws what they hear about each part of the face. Together the artist and describer use computers and photographs to help them pick and choose details. The final picture is not meant to look exactly like the person, but rather to remind other people of someone they've seen before.

Police Officer Eileen Bartosz's sketch of a robbery suspect is based on a witness's description.

Illustrators often have to follow an art director's instructions and get their approval on each step of an illustration's creation. Doing your best work while meeting a tight **deadline** is important to being a successful illustrator.

Most illustrators learn many **techniques**. They draw what they see and what they imagine. They use color, shadow, and design to tell the ideas in the words. Some use pencil, ink, or paint to create their illustrations. Others use computers to create or modify their work.

Sequential Artists

Sequential artists create a set of pictures that tell a story in order. Sometimes the pictures include words, such as in a comic book. Often a writer and an artist work together to decide how the story will unfold in the pictures.

Storyboards are sequential art. A storyboard artist works with a movie or television director to create a picture for each scene before it is filmed. Then the camera operator, actors, and director use these pictures as they film the show.

Storyboard for *Do Robots Get Spacesick?* Illustrated by Alex Lopez

These artists need a strong portfolio to show their computer and drawing skills. Storyboard artists need to know how to tell a story with pictures and how movies are made. It is essential that they are able to get along with the other creative people on the film's team. These artists need a strong portfolio to show their computer and drawing skills.

PORTFOLIOS

Illustrators and other artists need a portfolio to show art directors and potential clients what they can create. A portfolio contains copies of the artist's best works.

PRO ADVICE

"You need to learn to storytell with your drawings. That means figuring out how to put pictures together effectively on a page so that they relate your story to your readers. Look at the work of the storytellers you admire to begin to understand how visual storytelling can be accomplished, and then try your own hand at it with practice, practice, practice."

Walter Simonson, comic book illustrator

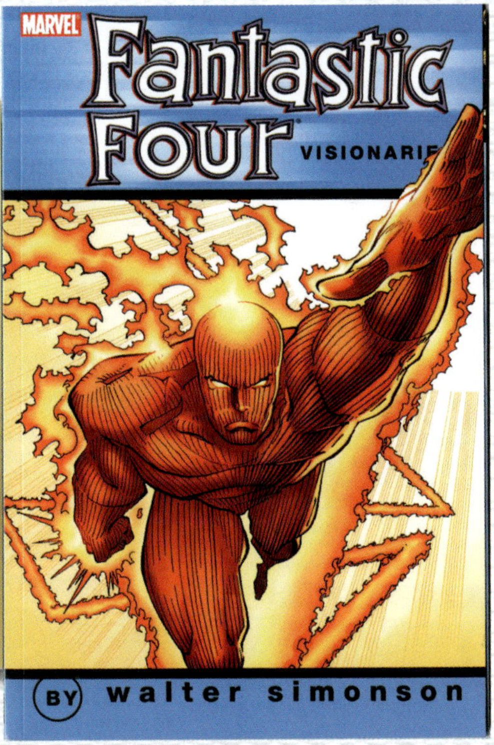

Comic artists draw comic books, graphic novels, comic strips, and webstrips. They tell a story by placing panels next to each other.

FREELANCERS

Many artists are freelancers who work at home. Freelancers run their own businesses. They must keep up with their taxes and expenses, buy health insurance, and find jobs. They sometimes work long hours to meet deadlines. Often they cannot predict what their income will be.

They need to know how to draw people, places, and things in the real world. These artists move the story along by designing the way panels are laid out on the page. After they have this foundation, some artists manipulate the drawing to create their own style. Sometimes they purposely change their subject so it does not look very realistic.

Many comic artists work with an editor, writer, penciller or inker, letterer, and colorist. Sometimes they are all the same person.

Sometimes comic book artists receive a story from a **publisher** and, once complete, it is published. Other artists create and draw their own story and then try to get it published.

DID YOU KNOW?!

Several specialists might work on the art of a comic book. A penciller draws the layout in pencil or on the computer from the writer's script. The inker takes that art and goes over it with ink or on the computer. They often add shadows and mood to the original art. The letterer fits the words on the page and creates special effects. A colorist takes the completed art and places color on it before it is printed.

Animators create a series of images, called frames. Each of these drawings is slightly different than the one before it. When these are quickly displayed one after another, they show movement. These sequential frames are used to create animated shows and movies, video games, and advertisements.

Pixar Animation Studios is where computer specialists joined with animators to create "Toy Story," the first full-length computer-animated movie.

DID YOU KNOW?!
Employment of animators is projected to grow 10 percent from 2016 to 2026, faster than the average for all occupations, according to the U.S. Bureau of Labor Statistics. This growth will be fueled by increased demand for animation and visual effects in movies, video games, and television.

Animators draw by hand or with a computer. They complete some frames and then computers fill in the frames between their drawings. The figures and backgrounds are often drawn by different artists and then put together by the computer.

FAST FACT:
Snow White was the first American animated feature film. It was released in 1938. It was hand-drawn by hundreds of artists, including 32 animators.

Artists in the World

Fashion designers create new looks in clothing. They must draw each piece so it can be produced. Costume designers work with actors and actresses to create clothes for television, film, and theater. Often they combine clothes they design and items already available.

Fashion designers draw what they are thinking, but also need to know if their design is practical to make. They need to know how to sew, make patterns, choose fabrics, and describe what they want.

PRO ADVICE

"Do everything you can that pertains to your field. I worked in retail, worked with an arts group to put on fashion shows, worked for free on small budget movies to learn costume design, did a community theater costume design gig...etc. You have to keep learning."

Leigh Anne Balzekas,
fashion designer

Colleen Atwood has an academy award for her costume designs for the movie Memoirs of a Geisha.

Costume designers research historical periods or foreign cultures so their costumes are accurate. They work with actors, directors, and writers to create an outfit that expresses a character's personality. They must do all this and stay within a budget.

Scientific and **technical** illustrators create drawings that help people understand complex ideas. These drawings must be accurate. These artists study science as well as art techniques.

Scientific artists often draw from life. Sometimes they draw the tiny things that can't be seen, even in a microscope. Other times the artist must draw a scientist's ideas of how things once were, such as how a dinosaur looked. Technical illustrators might draw exactly how a huge machine works. Their work might appear in scientific magazines or textbooks, in museums, on websites, or as part of instructions.

Most of these artists get jobs like other artists do, through networking. However, the Guild of Natural Science Illustrators runs a portfolio website at science-art.com to help connect these artists to jobs.

DID YOU KNOW?!

Many students study a specific subject before they become artists. They might study space, the human body, or even how cars work. Then they use their art skills to help others understand the complex ideas and relationships in that subject. Because they have studied the information, they can make their drawings accurate.

Art teachers teach students in schools, community centers, and private studios. Some teaching jobs may require a teaching **certificate**, which can be earned as part of a college degree program.

Art teachers help students learn basic and advanced techniques, explore different mediums, and find outlets to share their work.

An art therapist is trained in art and psychology. Therapy helps people cope with emotional and physical problems. Art therapists help people deal with their feelings by creating art.

Art therapists are certified by the Art Therapy Credentials Board (ATCB). These registered art therapists work with individuals and groups in nursing homes, prisons, hospitals, and community centers.

Art can help children express their feelings and increase their self-confidence.

Tattoo artists draw on people using specialized inks and needles. They need to draw well and to understand what the drawing will look like on a body's flexible skin.

Most states require students train for hours under a licensed tattoo artist and take special health classes to become licensed. Once licensed, a tattoo artist can open their own shop.

A tattoo artist may take many hours to draw a complex picture on a body's curves.

Tattoo artists sit still for a long time while they draw and ink tattoos. A tattoo artist's work becomes a permanent part of their client's body. It's important that it's done with precision and care.

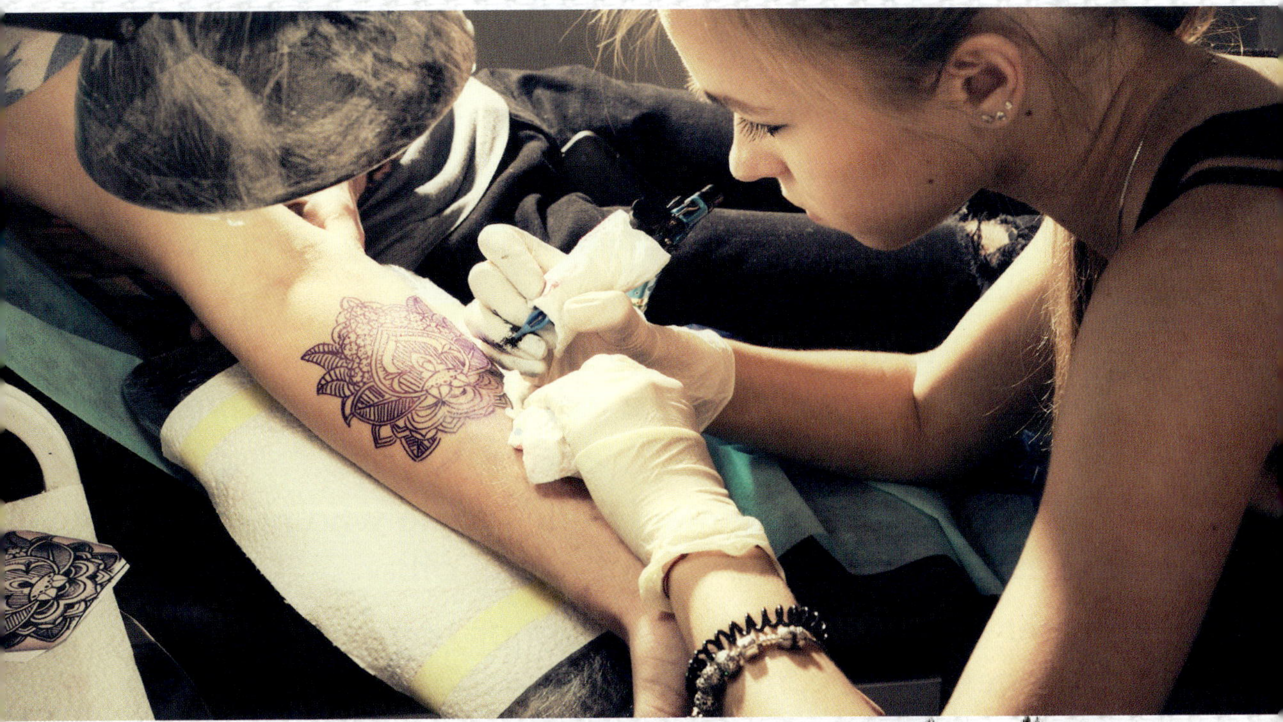

DID YOU KNOW?!

Famous tattoo artist Scott Campbell reportedly earns more than $1,000 for the first hour he works on a tattoo. His clients include a long list of celebrities. Before he became a tattoo artist, Scott was a biochemist!

Glossary

certificate (sur-TIF-uh-kit): a piece of paper that officially states that you are qualified to do something

conventions (kuhn-VEN-shuhns): formal gatherings of people who have the same profession or interests

deadline (DED-line): a time when something must be finished

freelancers (FREE-lans-urs): people who get paid for each individual job instead of earning a weekly salary as an employee of a company

galleries (GAL-ur-ees): places where paintings, sculptures, and other works of art are exhibited and sometimes sold

network (NET-wurk): to meet with people who share professional information with each other

publisher (PUHB-lish-ur): a person or company that produces a book, magazine, newspaper, or any other material so that many people can read it

sequential (SEE-kwen-shuhl): having a series of things that follow one another in a particular order

specialized (SPESH-uh-lized): focused on one area of work

technical (TEK-ni-kuhl): of or having to do with science, engineering, or the mechanical or industrial arts

techniques (tek-NEEKS): ways of doing something that requires skill, as in the arts, sports, or sciences

Index

Show What You Know

1. Which types of artists would most likely need to use computers?
2. What is the difference between the life of a freelance artist and one who is an employee of a company?
3. Why do artists need portfolios?
4. What are several things a teenager might do to learn about their chosen art career?
5. What are some basic skills that you can learn to prepare for almost any art career?

Further Reading

Crilley, Mark, *The Drawing Lesson: A Graphic Novel That Teaches You How to Draw*, Watson-Guptill, 2016.

Hart, Chris, *Fashion Design Studio: Learn to Draw Figures, Fashion, Hairstyles & More*, Drawing With Chris Hart, 2013.

Temple, Kathryn, *Art for Kids: Drawing: The Only Drawing Book You'll Ever Need to Be the Artist You've Always Wanted to Be*, Sterling Children's Books, 2014.

About the Author

Meet The Author!
www.meetREMauthors.com

Hilarie Staton is not an artist, but she is married to comic book artist Joe Staton. They live in an area that is filled with artists. Many of their friends are professional artists. She talked to many of them about their work as she researched this book. She wants to thank those who responded to her questions (there were many) and those whom she quotes: Jerry Craft, June Brigman, Karen O'Neil, Cindy Dill, Walter Simonson, and Leigh Anne Balzekas. They are all wonderful artists.

www.rourkeeducationalmedia.com

PHOTO CREDITS: Cover & Title Pg ©Nottomanv1, ©rusm, ©AlexD75, Pg 5, 7, 9, 11, 15, 22 ©MariatKary, Pg 3 ©ChrisAt, Pg 4 ©cokada, Pg 5 ©stellalevi, ©Picasa, Pg 6 ©eclipse_images, Pg 7 ©valentinrussanov, ©by Walt Simonson, Pg 8 ©bjones27, Pg 9 ©laflor, ©valentinrussanov, Pg 10 ©South_agency, Pg 11 ©shotsstudio, ©Picasa, Pg 12 ©Ed Simons/Alamy Stock Photo, Pg 13 ©ZUMA Press, Inc./Alamy Stock Photo, Pg 15 ©FILM STILLS/Alamy Stock Photo, Pg 16 ©mediaphotos, Pg 17 ©mediaphotos, Pg 18 ©mediaphotos, Pg 19 ©brytta, Pg 20 ©wiki, Pg 21 ©Moviestore collection Ltd/Alamy Stock Photo, Pg 22 ©scyther5, Pg 23 ©RGR Collection/Alamy Stock Photo, Pg 24 ©By tsaplia, Pg 25 ©Philartphace, Pg 26 ©monkeybusinessimages, Pg 27 ©Steve Debenport, Pg 28 ©baytunc, ©Oksana Pushenko, Pg 29 ©By Kathy Hutchins, ©LenaPar

Edited by: Keli Sipperley
Cover and Interior design by: Rhea Magaro-Wallace

Library of Congress PCN Data

An Artist / Hilarie Staton
(So You Wanna Be)
ISBN 978-1-64156-468-7 (hard cover)
ISBN 978-1-64156-594-3 (soft cover)
ISBN 978-1-64156-709-1 (e-Book)
Library of Congress Control Number: 2018930504

Rourke Educational Media
Printed in the United States of America,
North Mankato, Minnesota